AUDIO ACCESS INCLUDED

Two-Part Inventions
by J.S. Bach for Cello Duet

Arranged by

Audio arrangements performed by
Massimiliano Martinelli and Fulvia Mancini (Mr. & Mrs. Cello)

Sound Engineering: Eustacchio Montemurro – Audionova, Matera

To access audio visit:
www.halleonard.com/mylibrary

Enter Code
2701-3076-3101-5851

Photos by Ulrich Wydler

ISBN 978-1-70512-711-7

HAL•LEONARD®

Visit Hal Leonard Online at
www.halleonard.com

Contact us:
Hal Leonard
7777 West Bluemound Road
Milwaukee, WI 53213
Email: info@halleonard.com

In Europe, contact:
Hal Leonard Europe Limited
42 Wigmore Street
Marylebone, London, W1U 2RN
Email: info@halleonardeurope.com

In Australia, contact:
Hal Leonard Australia Pty. Ltd.
4 Lentara Court
Cheltenham, Victoria, 3192 Australia
Email: info@halleonard.com.au

Invention 1 in C Major

By JOHANN SEBASTIAN BACH
Arranged by Massimiliano Martinelli and Fulvia Mancini

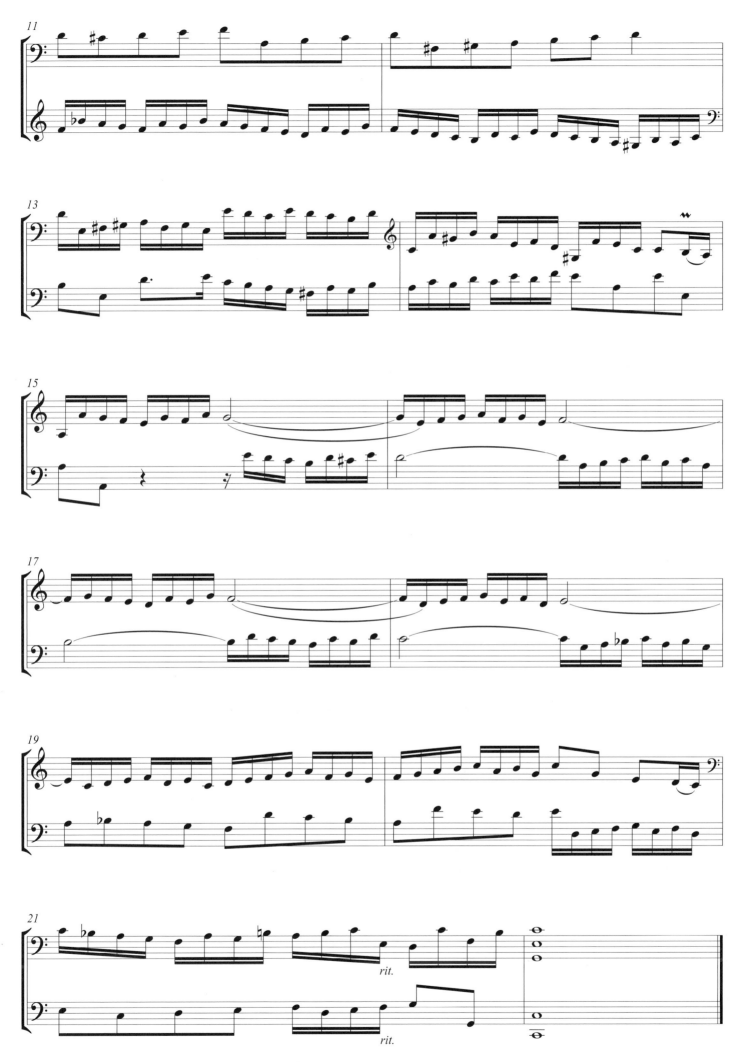

Invention 2 in C Minor

By JOHANN SEBASTIAN BACH

Arranged by Massimiliano Martinelli and Fulvia Mancini

Invention 3 in D Major

By JOHANN SEBASTIAN BACH

Arranged by Massimiliano Martinelli and Fulvia Mancini

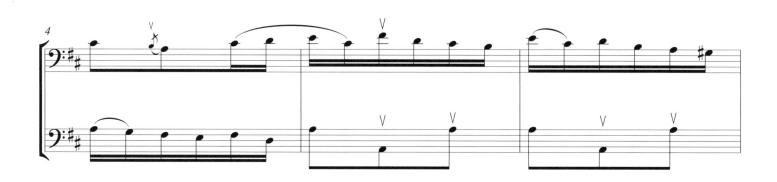

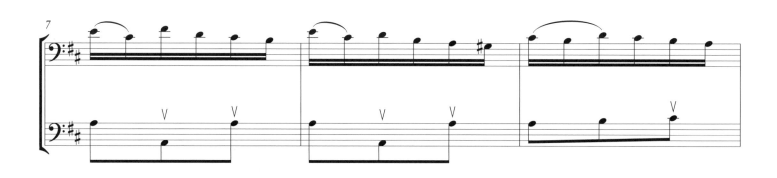

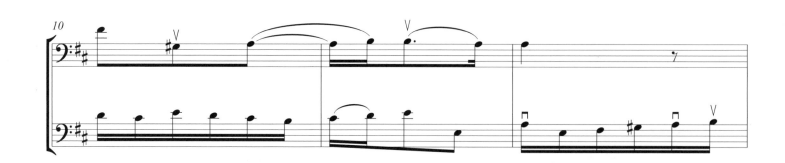

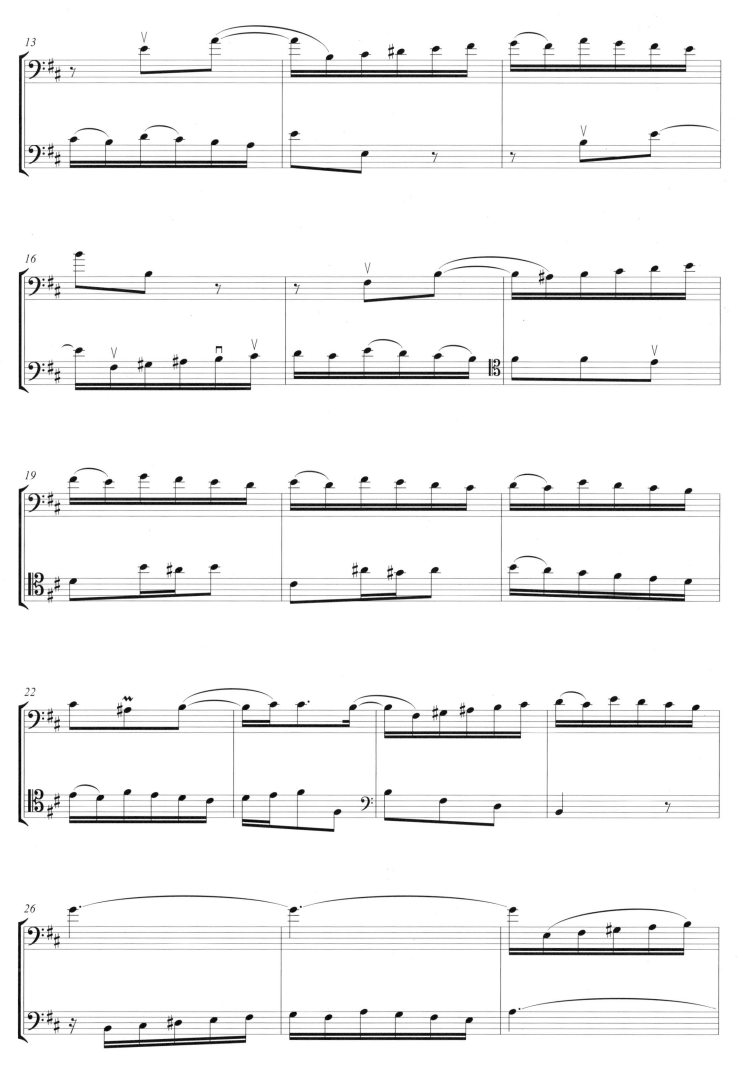

9

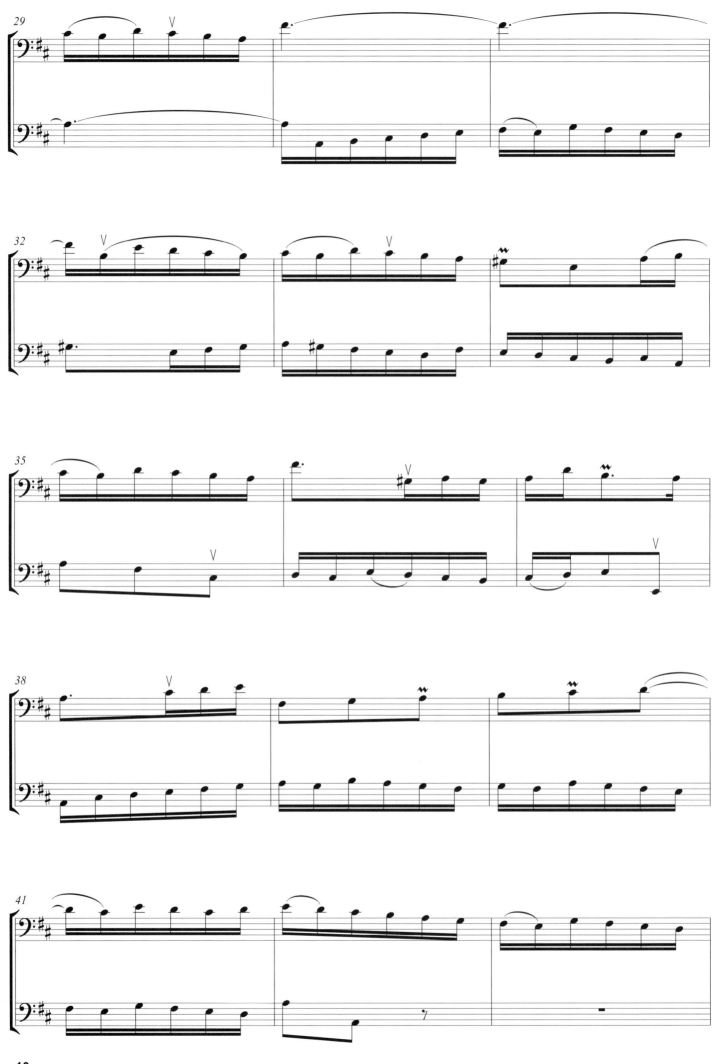

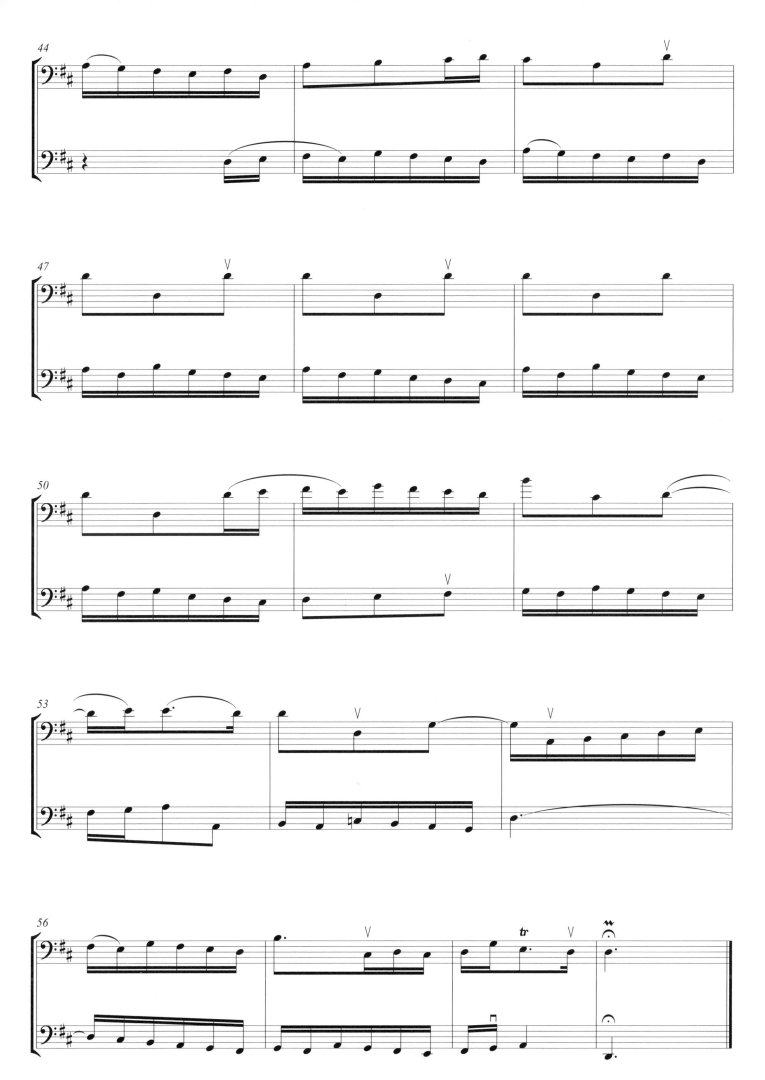

Invention 4 in D Minor

By JOHANN SEBASTIAN BACH
Arranged by Massimiliano Martinelli and Fulvia Mancini

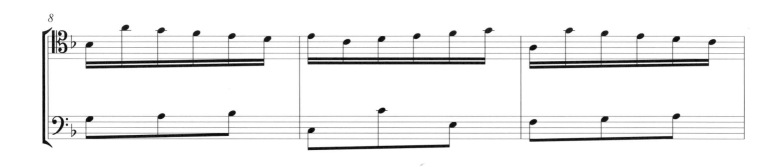

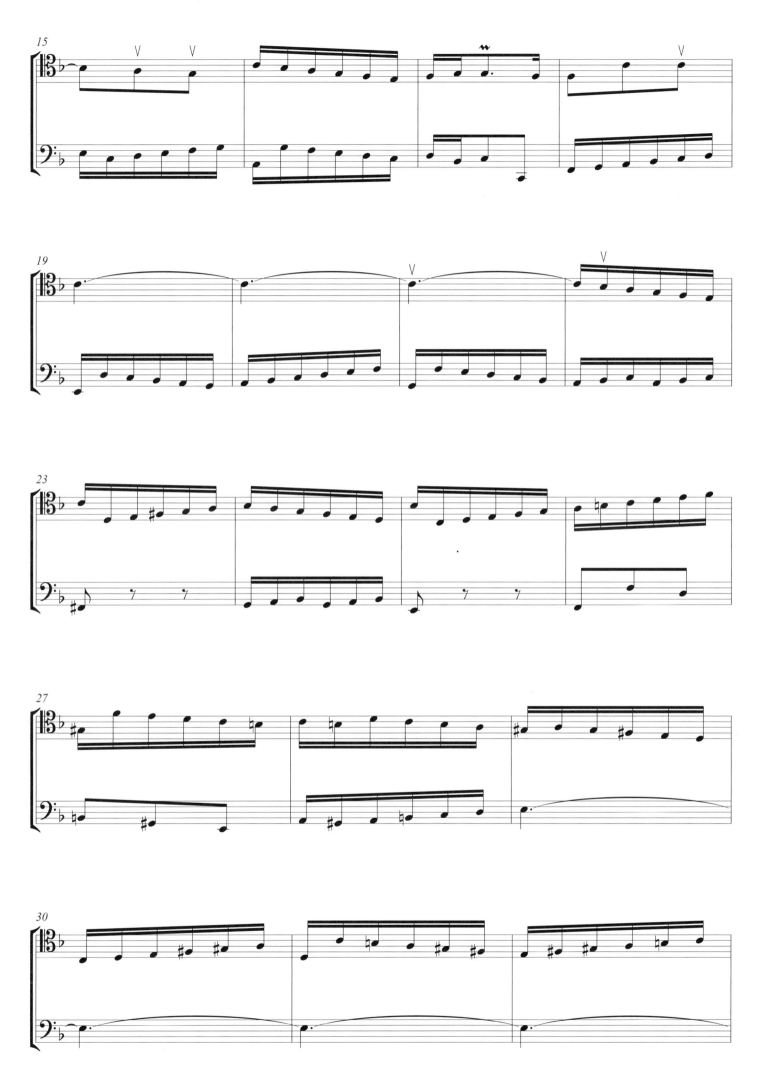

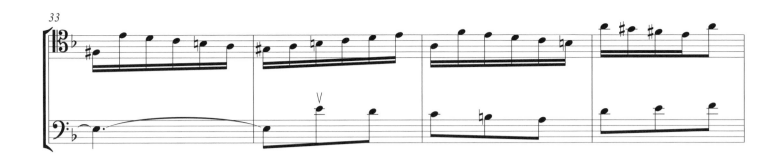

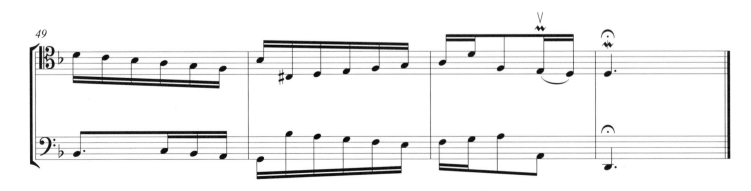

Invention 5 in E♭ Major

By JOHANN SEBASTIAN BACH

Arranged by Massimiliano Martinelli and Fulvia Mancini

Invention 6 in E Major

By JOHANN SEBASTIAN BACH

Arranged by Massimiliano Martinelli and Fulvia Mancini

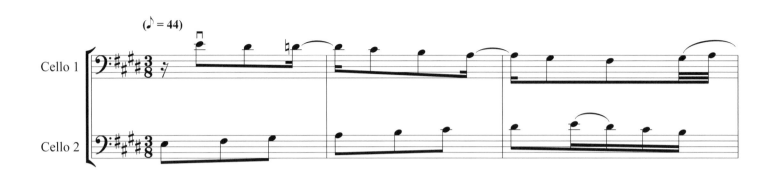

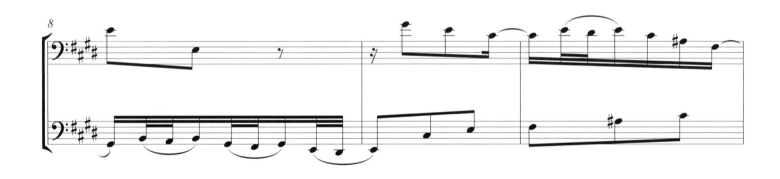

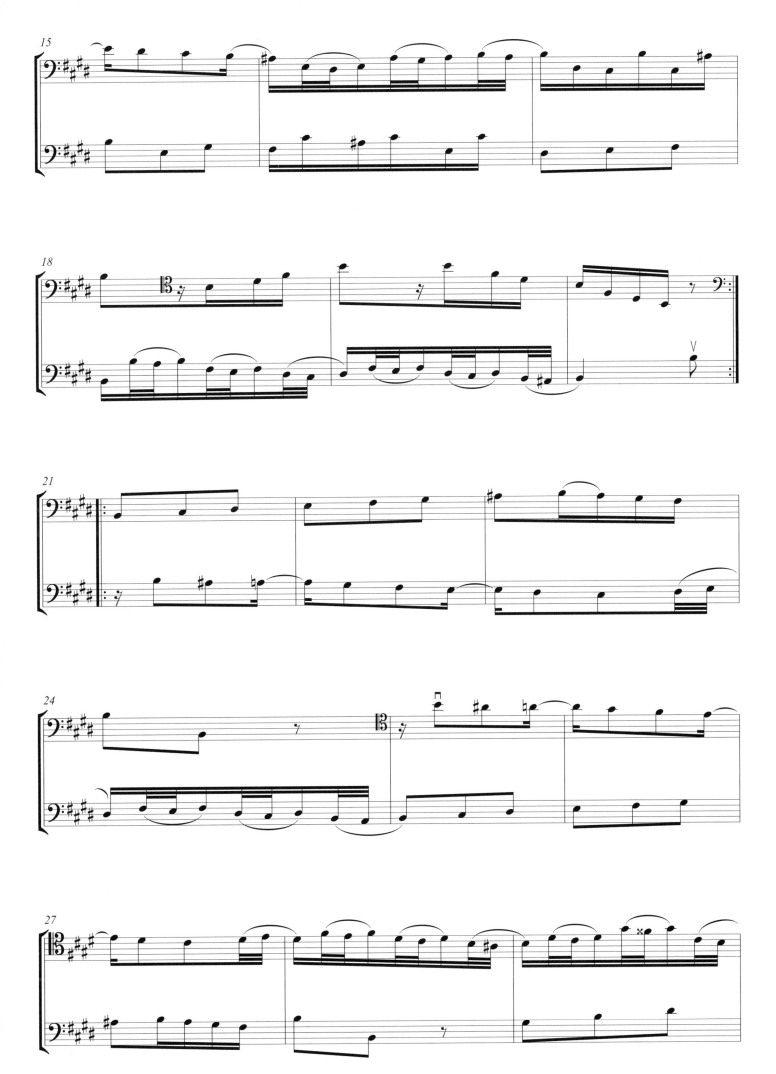

19

Two-Part Inventions
by J.S. Bach for Cello Duet

Arranged by **Mr & Mrs Cello**

Audio arrangements performed by
Massimiliano Martinelli and Fulvia Mancini (Mr. & Mrs. Cello)

Sound Engineering: Eustacchio Montemurro – Audionova, Matera

To access audio visit:
www.halleonard.com/mylibrary

Enter Code
5374-6108-2561-9438

ISBN 978-1-70512-711-7

Visit Hal Leonard Online at
www.halleonard.com

Contact us:
Hal Leonard
7777 West Bluemound Road
Milwaukee, WI 53213
Email: info@halleonard.com

In Europe, contact:
Hal Leonard Europe Limited
42 Wigmore Street
Marylebone, London, W1U 2RN
Email: info@halleonardeurope.com

In Australia, contact:
Hal Leonard Australia Pty. Ltd.
4 Lentara Court
Cheltenham, Victoria, 3192 Australia
Email: info@halleonard.com.au

Invention 1 in C Major

By JOHANN SEBASTIAN BACH
Arranged by Massimiliano Martinelli and Fulvia Mancini

Invention 2 in C Minor

By JOHANN SEBASTIAN BACH
Arranged by Massimiliano Martinelli and Fulvia Mancini

Cello 1

Cello 1

Invention 3 in D Major

By JOHANN SEBASTIAN BACH
Arranged by Massimiliano Martinelli and Fulvia Mancini

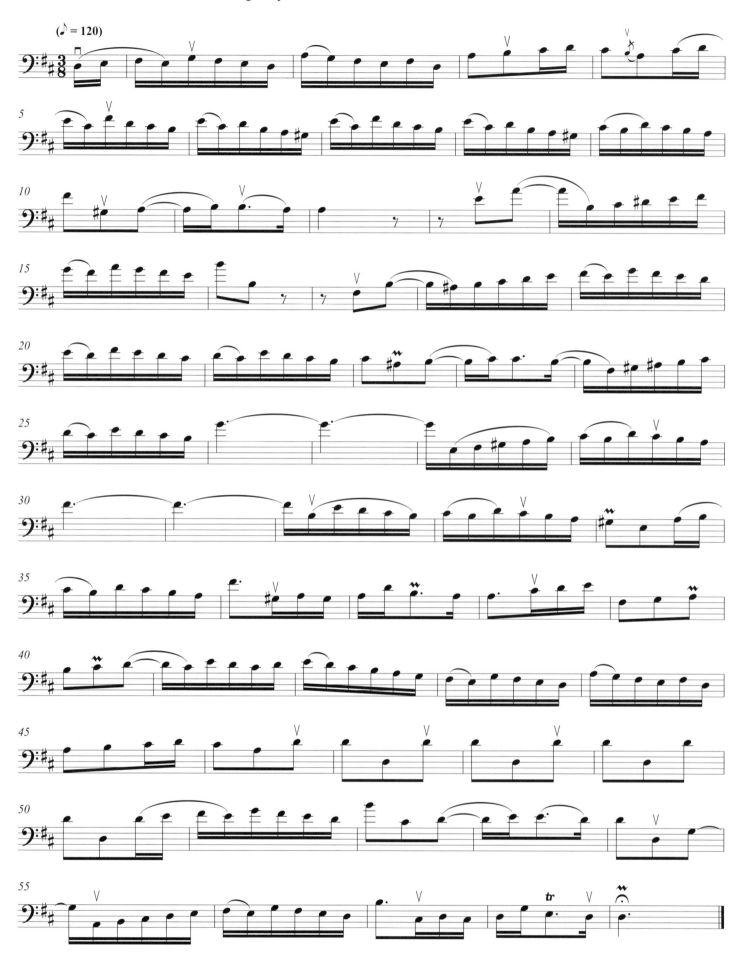

Invention 4 in D Minor

By JOHANN SEBASTIAN BACH
Arranged by Massimiliano Martinelli and Fulvia Mancini

Cello 1

Invention 5 in E♭ Major

By JOHANN SEBASTIAN BACH
Arranged by Massimiliano Martinelli and Fulvia Mancini

Cello 1

Invention 6 in E Major

By JOHANN SEBASTIAN BACH
Arranged by Massimiliano Martinelli and Fulvia Mancini

Cello 1

Invention 7 in E Minor

By JOHANN SEBASTIAN BACH
Arranged by Massimiliano Martinelli and Fulvia Mancini

Cello 1

Invention 8 in F Major

By JOHANN SEBASTIAN BACH
Arranged by Massimiliano Martinelli and Fulvia Mancini

Cello 1

Invention 9 in F Minor

By JOHANN SEBASTIAN BACH
Arranged by Massimiliano Martinelli and Fulvia Mancini

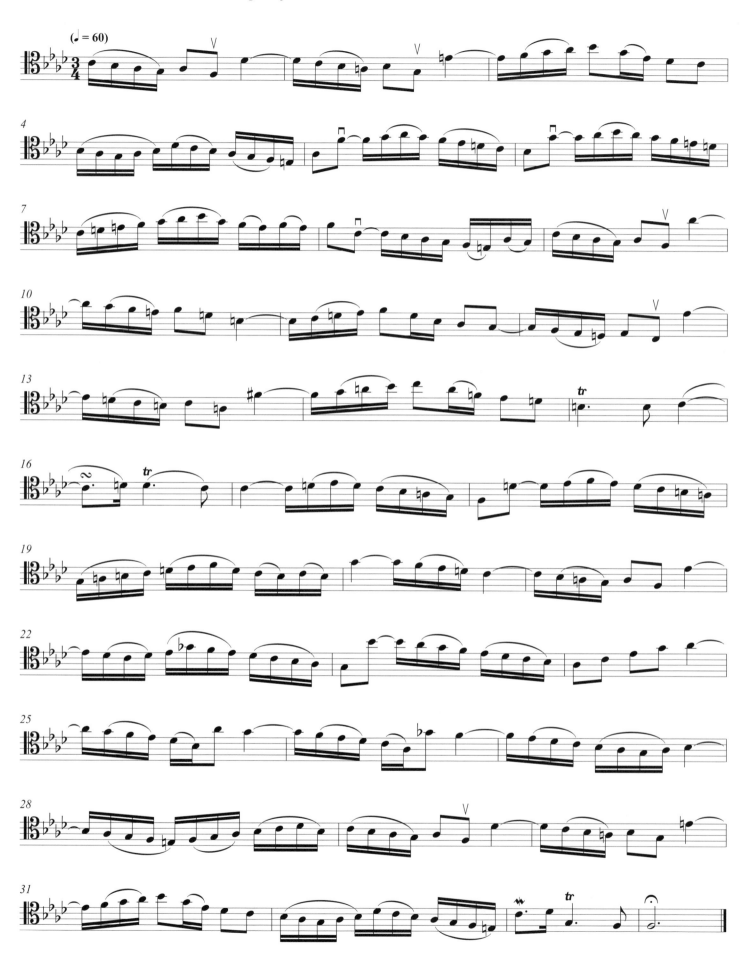

Invention 10 in G Major

By JOHANN SEBASTIAN BACH
Arranged by Massimiliano Martinelli and Fulvia Mancini

Cello 1

Invention 11 in G Minor

By JOHANN SEBASTIAN BACH
Arranged by Massimiliano Martinelli and Fulvia Mancini

Invention 12 in A Major

By JOHANN SEBASTIAN BACH
Arranged by Massimiliano Martinelli and Fulvia Mancini

Cello 1

Invention 13 in A Minor

By JOHANN SEBASTIAN BACH
Arranged by Massimiliano Martinelli and Fulvia Mancini

Cello 1

Invention 14 in B♭ Major
By JOHANN SEBASTIAN BACH
Arranged by Massimiliano Martinelli and Fulvia Mancini

Invention 15 in B Minor

By JOHANN SEBASTIAN BACH
Arranged by Massimiliano Martinelli and Fulvia Mancini

AUDIO ACCESS INCLUDED

Two-Part Inventions
by J.S. Bach for Cello Duet

Arranged by  Mr & Mrs Cello

Audio arrangements performed by
Massimiliano Martinelli and Fulvia Mancini (Mr. & Mrs. Cello)

Sound Engineering: Eustacchio Montemurro – Audionova, Matera

To access audio visit:
www.halleonard.com/mylibrary

Enter Code
7456-3412-3442-7176

ISBN 978-1-70512-711-7

Hal•Leonard®

Visit Hal Leonard Online at
www.halleonard.com

Contact us:
Hal Leonard
7777 West Bluemound Road
Milwaukee, WI 53213
Email: info@halleonard.com

In Europe, contact:
Hal Leonard Europe Limited
42 Wigmore Street
Marylebone, London, W1U 2RN
Email: info@halleonardeurope.com

In Australia, contact:
Hal Leonard Australia Pty. Ltd.
4 Lentara Court
Cheltenham, Victoria, 3192 Australia
Email: info@halleonard.com.au

Invention 1 in C Major

By JOHANN SEBASTIAN BACH

Arranged by Massimiliano Martinelli and Fulvia Mancini

Cello 2

Cello 2

Invention 2 in C Minor

By JOHANN SEBASTIAN BACH
Arranged by Massimiliano Martinelli and Fulvia Mancini

Invention 3 in D Major

By JOHANN SEBASTIAN BACH

Arranged by Massimiliano Martinelli and Fulvia Mancini

Cello 2

Invention 4 in D Minor

By JOHANN SEBASTIAN BACH
Arranged by Massimiliano Martinelli and Fulvia Mancini

Cello 2

Cello 2

Invention 5 in E♭ Major

By JOHANN SEBASTIAN BACH
Arranged by Massimiliano Martinelli and Fulvia Mancini

Cello 2

Invention 6 in E Major

By JOHANN SEBASTIAN BACH
Arranged by Massimiliano Martinelli and Fulvia Mancini

Invention 7 in E Minor

By JOHANN SEBASTIAN BACH
Arranged by Massimiliano Martinelli and Fulvia Mancini

Cello 2

Invention 8 in F Major

By JOHANN SEBASTIAN BACH

Arranged by Massimiliano Martinelli and Fulvia Mancini

Invention 9 in F Minor

By JOHANN SEBASTIAN BACH
Arranged by Massimiliano Martinelli and Fulvia Mancini

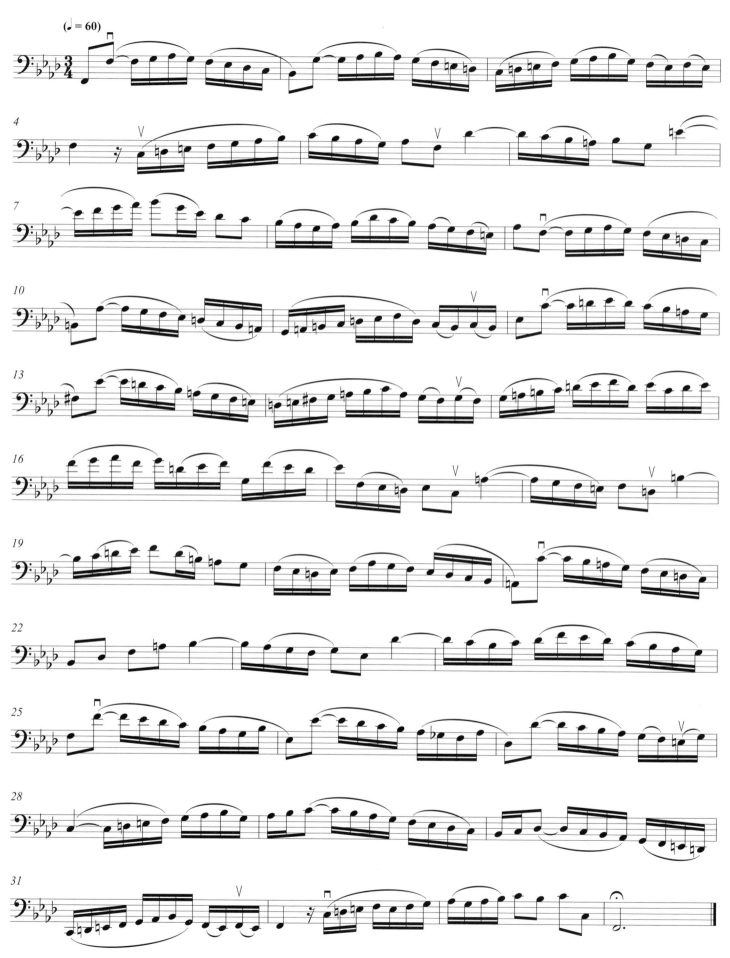

Cello 2

Invention 10 in G Major

By JOHANN SEBASTIAN BACH
Arranged by Massimiliano Martinelli and Fulvia Mancini

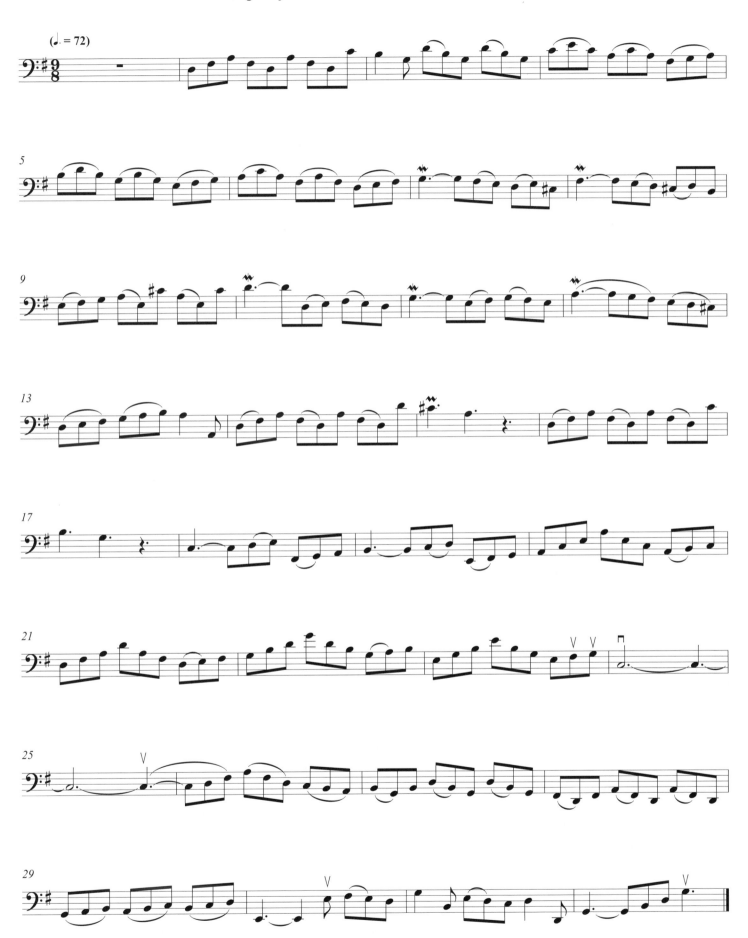

Invention 11 in G Minor

By JOHANN SEBASTIAN BACH
Arranged by Massimiliano Martinelli and Fulvia Mancini

Cello 2

Cello 2

Invention 12 in A Major

By JOHANN SEBASTIAN BACH
Arranged by Massimiliano Martinelli and Fulvia Mancini

Invention 13 in A Minor

By JOHANN SEBASTIAN BACH
Arranged by Massimiliano Martinelli and Fulvia Mancini

Cello 2

Invention 14 in B♭ Major

By JOHANN SEBASTIAN BACH

Arranged by Massimiliano Martinelli and Fulvia Mancini

Cello 2

Invention 15 in B Minor

By JOHANN SEBASTIAN BACH
Arranged by Massimiliano Martinelli and Fulvia Mancini

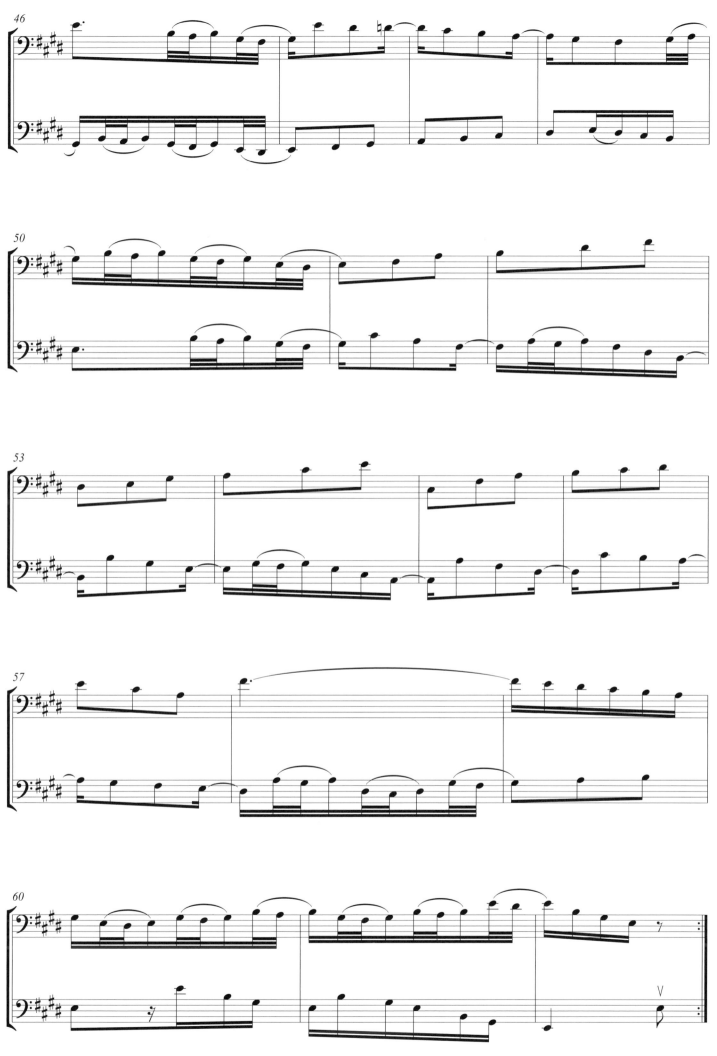

Invention 7 in E Minor

By JOHANN SEBASTIAN BACH
Arranged by Massimiliano Martinelli and Fulvia Mancini

Invention 8 in F Major

By JOHANN SEBASTIAN BACH

Arranged by Massimiliano Martinelli and Fulvia Mancini

Invention 9 in F Minor

By JOHANN SEBASTIAN BACH

Arranged by Massimiliano Martinelli and Fulvia Mancini

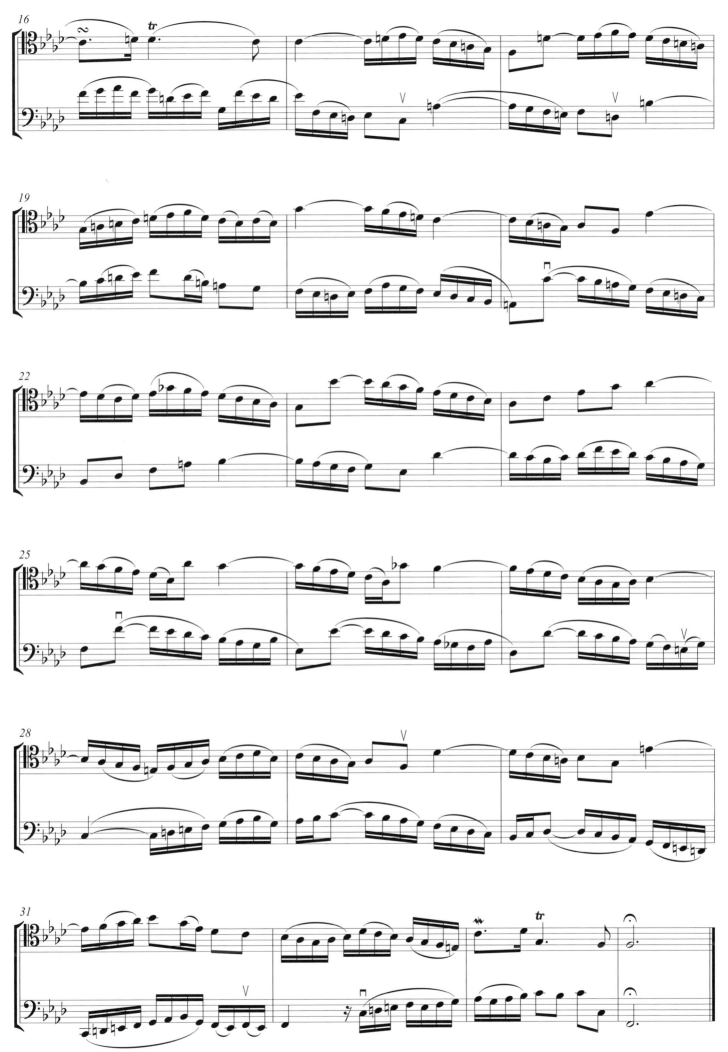

Invention 10 in G Major

By JOHANN SEBASTIAN BACH
Arranged by Massimiliano Martinelli and Fulvia Mancini

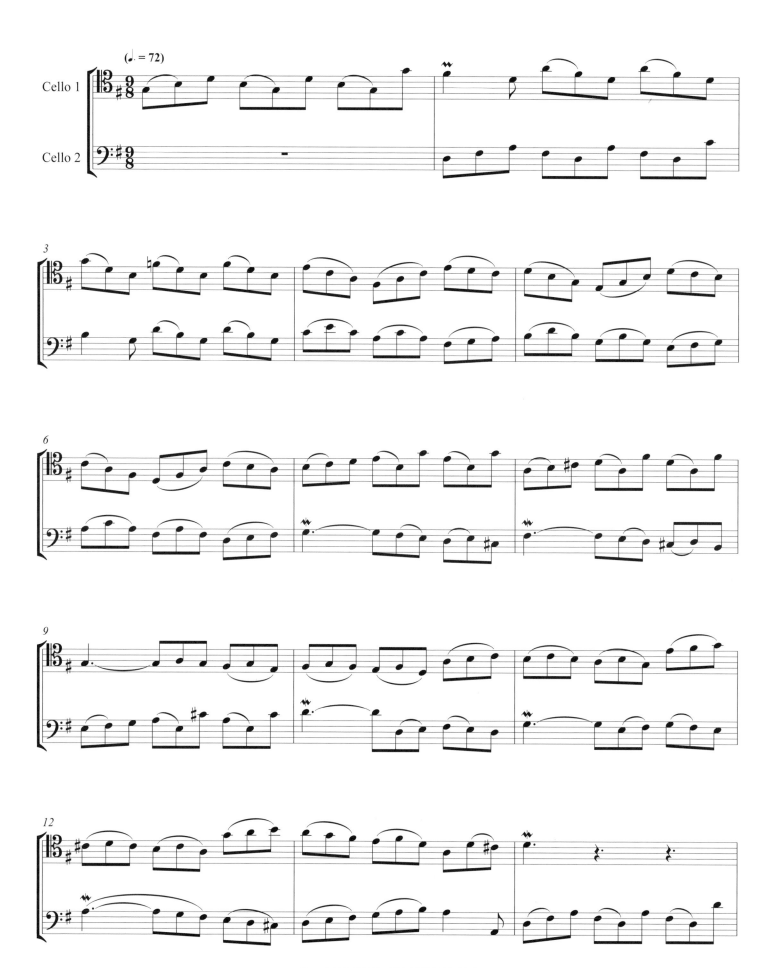

Invention 11 in G Minor

By JOHANN SEBASTIAN BACH

Arranged by Massimiliano Martinelli and Fulvia Mancini

Invention 12 in A Major

By JOHANN SEBASTIAN BACH
Arranged by Massimiliano Martinelli and Fulvia Mancini

Invention 13 in A Minor

By JOHANN SEBASTIAN BACH

Arranged by Massimiliano Martinelli and Fulvia Mancini

Invention 14 in B♭ Major

By JOHANN SEBASTIAN BACH

Arranged by Massimiliano Martinelli and Fulvia Mancini

Invention 15 in B Minor

By JOHANN SEBASTIAN BACH

Arranged by Massimiliano Martinelli and Fulvia Mancini